PEARL HARBOR

FOR KIDS

CHARLES MCKINNEY

Pearl Harbor

PEARL HARBOR

Enchanting United States History of Most Influential Events from Pearl Harbor

FOR KIDS

CHARLES MCKINNEY

DR. HISTORY

Don't Forget Your Free Bonus Downloads!

As our way of saying thank you, we've included in every purchase bonus gift downloads. If you've enjoyed reading this book, please consider leaving a review.

Or Scan Your Phone to open QR code

Pearl Harnbor:

Enchanting United States History of Most Influential Events from Pearl Harbor for Kids

Copyright © 2023 by Dr. History

Pearl Harbor

TABLE OF CONTENTS

Introduction. 9

Chapter 1:
    The Kingdom of Hawaii and
    the American's Arrival. 13

Chapter 2:
    Reciprocity Treaty of 1875
    and Pearl Harbor. 21

Chapter 3:
    Japan-American Relationship. 29

Chapter 4:
    Japan's Revived Hostility
    Toward Its Neighbors. 37

Chapter 5:
    Hatching Operation Z. 56

Chapter 6:
    The Passive American Defense. 53

Chapter 7:
    The Strike. 59

Chapter 8:
    Losses and Damage to Americans. 67

Chapter 9:
    Recovery of Pearl Harbor
    and Declaration of Wars. 75

Conclusion. 83

Bibliography. 86

About us. 88

Pearl Harbor

INTRODUCTION

"Let every man do his utmost duty."

– Admiral Heihachiro Togo

The history of war and humanity are closely connected. Without first knowing how war has impacted our lives, it is impossible to appreciate the modern world. We have all witnessed the consequences of conflict and the hardship they bring about.

Various factors can cause countries to go to war. It has been claimed that a nation will begin a conflict if it perceives the advantages of war exceed the downsides and there is no amicable way to resolve the dispute. The Japanese government thought that advancing on its neighbor's land and controlling its import market were the only ways to address the country's demographic and economic challenges.

American leaders implemented a number of trade restrictions and economic sanctions in response to this hostility. The sanctions strengthened the Japanese people's will to defend their position. The ability to fight is the single most crucial element in battle. The Japanese did not just have the willingness to fight for what they believed in; it was their enormous duty.

The Americans were also striving for what they thought was right. The only difference was that the Japanese also fought for their culture and against racism. They were fighting for equality. For years, Japan endured unequal treatment from western countries. The world's finest technology is useless without the willpower to use and continue utilizing it even as fatalities mount and unforeseen disasters occur. Perhaps, it was more personal for the Japanese. They had more of the human nature of war.

All conflicts and nearly all battles are decided by considerations of human will, with very few exemptions. It said that the secret to victory in war is to break the enemy's willpower while maintaining one's determination to fight. While America's economic sanctions on Japan could be categorized as breaking Japan's willpower, it has drawn a different result.

Fighting spirit stands for the indisputably human character of conflict. In the sections below, we will look into the origins of the battle; discover what fueled the fighting spirit of the Americans and Japanese. The factors that led the Japanese to carry out an almost impossible mission of attacking Pearl Harbor will be discussed below.

THE KINGDOM OF HAWAII AND THE AMERICAN'S ARRIVAL

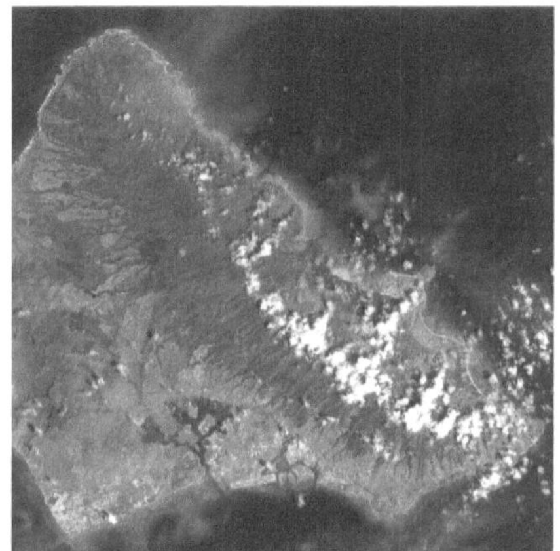

Pearl Harbor, the location of the Japanese air raid that brought America into World War II, may be seen on the bottom left side of the photo. The harbor continues to be a base for the US navy.

The Kingdom of Hawaii was flourishing and significant in 1795 due to agriculture and its advantageous location in the Pacific. Shortly after British explorer James Cook arrived on the island, American immigration, spearheaded by Protestant missionaries, and Native Hawaiian outmigration, primarily on whaling ships, started. Commencing with Kamehameha I's institution of the Kingdom of Hawaii in 1795, the Kamehameha dynasty ruled the nation.

In 1846, under the rule of Kamehameha III, Hawaii's independence was formally acknowledged by U.S. Secretary of State John C. Calhoun on behalf of President John Tyler. Following the declaration of Hawaiian independence, the Hawaiian Kingdom signed treaties with significant countries worldwide. It launched more than 90 legations and consulates in numerous seaports and towns.

Moreover, after Cook arrived, Hawaii's primary export was sugar. The first stable sugarcane plantation was established on the islands of Kauai in 1835. To grow sugar cane, William Hooper rented 980 acres (4 km2) of land from Kamehameha III. Plantations would exist on four of the major islands in thirty years. Hawaii's economy had been entirely changed by sugar. The Americans used agricultural techniques that demanded a significant amount of labor. To be employed in the fields, large numbers of permanent immigrants arrived from the Philippines, China, and Japan.

American plantation owners' insistence on representation in Kingdom politics marked the beginning of American influence on Hawaiian governance. The King and chiefs experienced pressure from these plantation owners in the form of requests for land ownership. The Great Mahele was Kamehameha III's response to the petitions, which distributed the lands to all Hawaiians.

During the Great Mahele of 1848, one-third of the land was given to monarchs, another third was divided among heads and land administrators, and the final third was distributed to the commoners. The Kuleana Act of 1850 mandated that land claims be submitted within two years, but many Hawaiians failed to do so. The Republic's administration subsequently sold most of the property to Americans from other parts of the country or auctioned it off to The Big Five (Hawaii) firms. The Big Five were a group of businesses that began as sugarcane processing companies and had significant political influence.

On July 10, 1850, the legislature enacted the Alien Land Ownership Act when opposition Kamehameha IV, Kamehameha V, and missionary physician Gerrit Judd were overseas. The law made it possible for non-citizens to own land. William Little Lee, the Chief Justice, authored the Act. William Lee was an American attorney who served as the first chief justice of the Kingdom of Hawaii's Supreme Court. The promise of wealth brought on by an inflow of greatly needed capital and workers served as the basis for the law.

Moreover, in the 1850s, Kamehameha III sought reciprocity because Hawaii's import taxes on sugar were significantly more outstanding. On the other hand, the Hawaiians were charging a cheaper import tax to the United States. The King wanted to make Hawaiian sugar compete with other countries by reducing American tariffs. Kamehameha III advocated reciprocity between the nations in 1854, but the United States Senate rejected the idea.

The Kamehameha Dynasty ruled the Kingdom of Hawaii from 1795 to 1874. The first elected ruler of the Hawaiian Kingdom was William Charles Lunalilo, who would also be the last leader of the Kamehameha dynasty. Lunalilo, as monarch, was satisfied to let Charles Reed Bishop handle the majority of commercial activities, but Hawaiians opposed the cession of territory. Bishop was a foreigner who wedded into the Kamehameha family and later became the Minister of Foreign Affairs for Hawaii and lived in a rural area close to Pu'uloa.

The 39-year-old Lunalilo passed away on February 3, 1874, without designating an heir. His attempt to cancel all negotiations on ceding of lands eventually failed. The constitution granted the legislature the authority to choose the monarch in these circumstances. The legislature resolved to have a public vote and to pick the candidates. Both David Kalakaua and Queen Emma, wife of the late Kamehameha IV, proclaimed their candidacy.

David Kalakaua was elected King. However, Queen Emma and her allies were not pleased, marched to the capitol, and aggressed the lawmakers. The Hawaiian administration asked American forces to help end the violence because the monarchy lacked an army, and the police had fled. The legislature then appropriately chose Kalakaua to succeed Lunalilo.

The reign of the Kalakaua Dynasty began with King David Kalakaua's ascending the throne in 1874. The dynasty would last until the downfall of Queen Lili'uokalani in 1893. Thus, the dynasty's main line ended when the ousted Queen Liliuokalani (who had resigned and stepped down) passed away in 1917.

Fun Fact:

Japanese in Hawaii. There were 153 Japanese deployed to Hawaii. They were the initial group of Japanese immigrants authorized to be employed on Hawaii's sugarcane plantation on Kauai, Maui, Lanai, and Oahu. By 1896, the Japanese made up around 25% of the Hawaiian population. The Japanese government structured and provided them with specific protection.

Fun Fact:

The First Elected Ruler. William Charles Lunalilo served as the Kingdom of Hawaii's sixth king. American missionaries taught the grandnephew of King Kamehameha I and a member of the royal family, Lunalilo, at the Royal School before King Kamehameha III declared him qualified for succession. The kingdom's legislature unanimously elected him to the throne in 1873.

Trivia Questions:

1. When was the Kingdom of Hawaii instituted?

2. Who was the first monarch in the Kingdom?

3. What was Hawaii's primary export?

4. Who was the next reigning family after the Kamehameha?

5. Who was Hawaii's first elected ruler?

Answers:

1. When was the Kingdom of Hawaii instituted? **1795**
2. Who was the first monarch in the Kingdom? **Kamehameha I**
3. What was Hawaii's primary export? **sugar**
4. Who was the next reigning family after the Kamehameha? **The Kalakaua**
5. Who was Hawaii's first elected ruler? **William Charles Lunalilo**

RECIPROCITY TREATY OF 1875 AND PEARL HARBOR

Upon King David Kalakaua's reign, the U.S. government coerced the new leader to turn over Pearl Harbor to the Navy. Kalakaua feared this would result in a takeover by the United States and violate Hawaiian customs, which held that the land was fertile, pure, and not for trade. The control of Hawaii by the United States was deemed essential for the security of its west coast. Pu'uloa, Pearl Harbor, piqued the interest of the military in particular. Charles Reed Bishop advocated selling one harbor.

Pearl Harbor is on Oahu, west of Honolulu, Hawaii. A sizable shallow embayment served as Pearl Harbor's original form. The Hawaiians called it Wai Momi, Hawaiian for "Waters of Pearl," or Pu'uloa, Hawaiian for "long hill." Tradition has it that the powerful Ewa chief Keaunui has established a passable waterway close to the present-day Pu'uloa saltworks. The channel allowed for transportation within the estuary known as the "Pearl River."

Lacking significant depth, Pearl Harbor was seldom used for huge ships throughout the early nineteenth century. Due to its whale hunting, shipping, and trade operations in the Pacific, the United States developed an increased interest in the Hawaiian Islands. A large number of American warships visited Honolulu in the 1820s and 1830s. The commanding troops typically carried letters from the United States Government guiding on matters related to the island nation's ties with other countries. The Honolulu-based Polynesian newspaper called for the establishment of a naval post in Hawaii in 1841 to protect American whaling business workers.

A United States military commission proposed to acquire Ford Island (Pearl Harbor) in compensation for America's ability to import sugar tax-free as early as 1873. The Reciprocity Treaty of 1875, signed and ratified in 1875, was officially a free trade agreement that governed the dealings of the United States of America and the Hawaiian Kingdom. For seven years, it permitted tax-free entry into the United States of several Hawaiian products, namely sugar and rice. In exchange, Hawaii consented not to impose import tariffs on items made in the United States that enter Hawaii.

Although not all Hawaiians favored the agreement, it became a reality a year after Kalakaua's victory. Beginning in September 1876, the treaty allowed full access to the American market for sugar and other goods produced in the Kingdom of Hawaii. In exchange, the U.S. received land in the Pu'uloa region for what would eventually become the Pearl Harbor naval base. The agreement spurred significant American investment in sugarcane farms in Hawaii. Joseph Nawahi, a lawmaker from Hawaii, asserted that the deal would be a nation-seizing treaty.

The United States started renting Pearl Harbor on January 20, 1887. Shortly after, the Hawaiian Patriotic League, a party of primarily non-Hawaiians, launched the Rebellion of 1887. On July 6, 1887, the group penned its own constitution. Lorrin Thurston, the Hawaiian Minister of Interior who utilized the Hawaiian army to threaten Kalakaua, was responsible for writing the new regulations. King Kalakaua was coerced and threatened into signing the new charter known as the Bayonet Constitution. The constitution favored foreign plantation owners while significantly reducing the King's power.

Moreover, the new constitution gave the King the authority to choose Cabinet Ministers. Still, it prohibited him from removing them without the Legislature's consent. Since the Legislature is now in charge of naturalizing aliens, Americans and Europeans could continue to hold their national citizenship and exercise their right to vote. Further, Americans had the right to vote and occupy public office while still being citizens of the United States. Any other country did not offer this privilege, and they may even vote before obtaining naturalization. These events led to the Wilcox Rebellion of 1888. The rebellion attempted to depose King David Kalakaua and replace him with his sister.

When Kalakaua passed away in 1891, her sister Queen Lili'uokalani took over as monarch. The main goal of Lili'uokalani was to establish a new constitution and revoke the 1887 Bayonet Constitution to give the monarchy back its authority. Many non-citizen Americans and Europeans would have lost their citizenship as a result. The attempt by Lili'uokalani to enact a new constitution on January 14, 1893, catalyzed the downfall of the Hawaiian Kingdom three days later. Five Americans, one Englishman, and one German national comprised the perpetrators, led by Thurston. Further, John L. Stevens, a diplomat in the U.S. government, backed the coup exploits.

Republican expansionist William McKinley succeeded Democrat Grover Cleveland as President of the United States in March 1897. On July 7, 1898, McKinley approved the Newlands Resolution annexing Hawaii, establishing the Territory of Hawaii. In 1899, the United States Navy built a station on Pearl Harbor after the overthrow of the Hawaiian Kingdom.

Fun Fact:

Wilcox Rebellion of 1888. Robert William Wilcox was a native Hawaiian officer who was Kalakaua's distant cousin. When the support for his study program was cut off, he returned to Hawaii in October 1887 at the same time as Liliuokalani. Sam Nowlein, Charles B. Wilson, Princess Lili'uokalani, and Wilcox hatched a scheme to depose King Kalakaua and install Lili'uokalani.

Fun Fact:

Kalakaua's Secret Meeting with the Japanese Emperor. Kalakaua was apprehensive about the possibility of the United States taking the Hawaiian Islands. To bring Hawaii under the protection of Japan, Kalakaua met with the Japanese Emperor in secret on his 1881 overseas trip. He suggested an arranged marriage between his 5-year-old niece Princess Ka'iulani and 13-year-old Prince Yamashina Sadamaro would bring the two countries together. However, his proposal was rejected.

Fill in the blanks to complete the story.

Pearl Harbor is on Oahu, west of Honolulu, _______. Lacking significant ______, Pearl Harbor was seldom used for huge ______ throughout the early nineteenth century. The United States started renting Pearl Harbor on _______. In 1899, the _______ built a station on Pearl Harbor after the overthrow of the Hawaiian Kingdom.

Answers:

Pearl Harbor is on Oahu, west of Honolulu, **Hawaii**. Lacking significant **depth**, Pearl Harbor was seldom used for huge **ships** throughout the early nineteenth century. The United States started renting Pearl Harbor on **January 20, 1887**. In 1899, the **United States Navy** built a station on Pearl Harbor after the overthrow of the Hawaiian Kingdom.

JAPAN-AMERICAN RELATIONSHIP

Pearl Harbor on December 7, 1941, when Japan launched a devastating surprise offensive on the US Pacific Fleet. During the assault, two bombs and six torpedoes sank West Virginia.

The shogun declared Japan a closed country in the 1600s after a number of Catholic missionaries had emerged and attempted to convert the inhabitants. The Japanese military tyrants were known as shoguns. In the 1800s, the US President also wanted entry to Japan at the same time as the American's arrival in Hawaii. Commodore Matthew Calbraith Perry, the pioneer of the American steam navy and the commandant of Brooklyn's New York Naval Shipyard, first arrived in Tokyo Bay in 1853. Commodore Perry brought with him the seven cannon-brandished warships of the East India Squadron, a white flag, US marines' troops, and a letter from President Millard Fillmore.

In order to expand American whaling and trade operations internationally, President Fillmore desired economic access to Japan. Whaling is the practice of hunting whales for their useful byproducts, such as flesh and fat, which may then be processed into a type of oil that gained importance during the Industrial Revolution. The letter also made the threat that Japan would be destroyed if American admission was denied.

The shogun signed an agreement adhering to Fillmore's demands realizing that he could not succeed. Many Japanese people, especially a group of young samurai known as shishi, Japanese for "men of great purpose," refused to recognize the forceful existence of foreign intruders in the years that followed. The shishi thought that these circumstances demonstrated a failing civilization and that the only way to restore culture was through a bloody revolution that would result in the killing or deportation of foreigners and the overthrow of the governing clan.

With the sudden death of Emperor Komei, Mutsuhito, at only 15, assumed the throne. Following his coronation as Meiji, the emperor employed foreigners to construct manufacturing facilities, railways, spinning mills, and port infrastructure. He served as the face of the Meiji Restoration, a wave of quick changes that saw feudal, isolated Japan become a major industrial nation. Emperor Meiji relocated his palace from Kyoto to Edo (present Tokyo), eradicated the feudal system, and established a constitutional government with a cabinet and legislature.

Japanese experienced a cultural revolution as more and more Western technology, industry, and culture proliferated. Outstanding Tokyo students studied seafaring and navigation in London, legislation in Paris, medical science in Germany, and economics in the United States. Further, Japan then defeated both Russia and China in its first two wars. The Japanese Imperial Navy employed its acquired 12-inch guns from England in its war with the Russian czar. A nation from Asia completely destroyed a European Navy for the first time in contemporary history.

After Japan defeated Russia at Tsushima, they anticipated receiving bounty settlements. However, the peace settlement arbitrated by Theodore Roosevelt upset the conquerors because they were denied Manchurian land or compensation. Manchuria was a known region in northeastern China. The Washington Naval Conference of 1922 came next, and it was an agreement that compelled Tokyo to accept a 10:10:6 ratio of the US, UK, and Japan's capacity for warships and aircraft carriers. This compromise was perceived by many Japanese officials as evidence that their nation would never be treated equally by Britain and America. This was the birth of Japan's indignation toward the United States.

In 1923, Ten percent of California's agriculture was grown by Japanese immigrant farmers on just one percent of the state's farmland. However, Japanese people were not permitted to own property in America under the constitution. Moreover, Japanese immigrants were prohibited from becoming citizens of the US, according to a decision made by the US Supreme Court a year earlier. In 1924, fifteen newspapers in Tokyo attacked America for his disparaging behavior after Congress implemented national immigration restrictions, with a quota for Japan of zero. Soon after, the United States was declared the primary enemy by the Imperial National Defense Policy of the Japanese Army and Navy General Staff.

Simultaneously, Japan perceived herself as surrounded by American and European colonies while feeling insulted by them. The British controlled Hong Kong, the Malay Peninsula, Singapore, and a portion of Shanghai; the Germans ruled China's Shandong Province; the French ruled a portion of Shanghai; the Dutch held enormous holdings in the East Indies; and the Americans controlled Hawaii, Midway, Guam, and the Philippines.

Even though Tokyo was given the German territories of Tsingtao, the Marianas, the Carolinas, and the Marshall Islands after winning the Great War, Japanese leaders would nevertheless condemn this foreign barricade in the years before Pearl Harbor. She was on her way to becoming an empire because of her military prowess, which earned her control of Korea, Taiwan, Sakhalin, the Ryukyus, the Bonins, the Pescadores, and the Kuril Islands.

Fun Fact:

The Russians raised three flags before the Japanese stopped firing at them. During the war between Japan and Russia in 1905, the six surviving Russian ships were given a surrender order. Russians waved XGE flags, an international surrender signal, but it was unknown to the Japanese, so they continued firing. Thus, a white tablecloth was placed up their flagpoles, yet the Japanese still kept on firing. The Russians finally came to a full halt, raising Japanese naval flags to their mastheads as a gesture of absolute submission.

Fun Fact:

The Great Pacific War Novel. Hector C. Bywater, a naval correspondent for the London Daily Telegraph, published a book titled The Great Pacific War in 1925. Bywater's book depicted a simultaneous Japanese assault on Guam and the Philippines that occurred alongside an unforeseen attack on the American navy in Pearl Harbor. Although there is no evidence linking this book to Japanese military strategy, it accurately predicted what would occur in the final weeks of 1941.

Match Phrases

Emperor of Japan

A group of young samurai

Japanese military tyrants

A region in northeastern China

Words: shogun, Manchuria, Mutsuhito, shishi

Answers:

Emperor of Japan - **Mutsuhito**

A group of young samurai - **shishi**

Japanese military tyrants - **shogun**

A region in northeastern China - **Manchuria**

JAPAN'S REVIVED HOSTILITY TOWARD ITS NEIGHBORS

General Douglas MacArthur, President Franklin D. Roosevelt,
and Admiral Chester W. Nimitz, in Pearl Harbor 1944.

Japan's aggressively expansionist goals in the 1930s resumed its tensions with its neighbors, China and Russia. Japan had previously won the war against China and Russia. Japan's imperialist aspirations sparked both conflicts. As a result, Japan established a sizable area of influence in Manchuria and saw a chance to extend its position in China.

Japan was denounced internationally for conquering Manchuria. In retaliation, Japan left the League of Nations in

1933. The League of Nations was the pioneer global intergovernmental body whose primary goal was to uphold international peace. Further, Japan pulled out of the Second London Naval Disarmament Conference in 1936 since the US and UK would not treat the Japanese Navy equally. The Second London Naval Disarmament Conference took place in London, United Kingdom. It led to the signing of the Second London Naval Treaty international agreement.

In 1937, the Marco Polo Bridge Incident denoted the start of a second conflict between Japan and China. Similarly, the United States and several League of Nations members, including Britain, France, Australia, and the Netherlands, criticized Japan's 1937 war on China. Japanese wartime crimes, such as the infamous Nanking Massacre that December, furthered tensions with the rest of the globe. Following the Battle of Nanking in the Second Sino-Japanese War, the Imperial Japanese Army conducted mass execution of Chinese citizens in Nanjing, the Republic of China's capital.

Each country had colonies in East and Southeast Asia: the U.S., Britain, France, and the Netherlands. These Western economic and territorial interests in Asia were endangered by Japan's increasing military strength and her willingness to use it. In 1938, the United States implemented a series of more severe trade restrictions with Japan. These attempts to stop Japan from continuing its war in China were unsuccessful.

In 1940, the Axis Powers were formally established when Japan joined the Tripartite Pact with Hitler's Germany and Dictatorial Italy. A military alliance known as the Axis Powers instituted World War II and battled the Allies. Hitler's Germany, the Kingdom of Italy, and the Japanese Empire comprised its founding members. The Tripartite Pact was largely aimed at the United States and was a defensive military agreement.

Hitler's war in Europe would serve Japan's purposes in advancing its goals in the Far East. The Tripartite Pact assured support if a signatory was threatened by any country that had not been at war with the signatory; this implied the United States. To intimidate Japan, President Franklin D. Roosevelt relocated the US Pacific Fleet to Pearl Harbor in the middle of 1940. America gradually transitioned from being a neutral power to one getting ready for war due to its commitment to aiding the British and Chinese.

The United States increased its efforts to restrict Japan economically as a result of Japan's actions. The restrictions included blocking the flow of scrap metal to Japan and banning Japanese ships from using the Panama Canal, which had a particularly detrimental effect on Japan's economy. Furthermore, on July 26, 1941, the US suspended Japanese resources and banned Japan's import of fuel and oil. Japan's most essential commodity at the time was oil, which at over 80% supplied by the United States. Following the economic sanctions, Kichisaburo Nomura, Japan's ambassador to Washington, and US Secretary of State, Cordell Hull, convened a series of discussions to address Japanese-American relations.

Fun Fact:

Saving Jewish Refugees. Japan's delegate to the League of Nations was Foreign Minister to Japan Yosuke Matsuoka. Due to poverty, he was cared for by Methodist missionaries in Portland, Oregon. Although he avoided poverty, he encountered racism. He rose to become Japan's Foreign Minister. He was instrumental in bringing Tokyo, Berlin, and Rome together through the Tripartite Pact. Ironically, he would provide shelter for Jewish refugees in Japanese-controlled Shanghai in 1938.

Fun Fact:

The United States' natural allies. In the struggle against global tyranny, 80% of Americans saw the Chinese as their natural allies, according to a 1938 poll. US missionaries have been traveling China for decades in search of Christian converts. This extensive network of Christian missionaries and their domestic fundraising efforts steadfastly portrayed China as a diligent and sincere younger sibling attempting to emulate America's democratic traditions.

Complete the Sentences

1. Japan's aggressive _______ goals in the 1930s resumed its tensions with its neighbors.

A. friendly　　　　B. expansionist　　　　C. economist

2. Japan was denounced internationally for conquering ______.

A. Manchuria　　　　B, China　　　　C.Philippines

3. The __________ Conference took place in London, United Kingdom.

A. Tripartite Pact　　　　B. League of Nations　　　　C. Second London Naval Disarmament

4. In 1940, the Axis Powers was formally established when Japan joined the __________.

A. Tripartite Pact　　　　B. League of Nations　　　　C. Second London Naval Disarmament

5. Americans saw the ______ as their natural allies, according to a 1938 poll.

A. Philippines　　　　B. Chinese　　　　C.Japanese

Answer:

1. Japan's aggressive _______ goals in the 1930s resumed its tensions with its neighbors.

B. expansionist

2. Japan was denounced internationally for conquering _______.

A. Manchuria

3. The __________ Conference took place in London, United Kingdom.

C. Second London Naval Disarmament

4. In 1940, the Axis Powers was formally established when Japan joined the __________.

A. **Tripartite** Pact

5. Americans saw the ______ as their natural allies, according to a 1938 poll.

B. Chinese

HATCHING OPERATION Z

Admiral Isoroku Yamamoto planned the assault on Pearl Harbor. Yamamoto wrote a letter to Navy Minister Koshiro Oikawa in January 1941 from his quarters on board the 32,000-ton battleship Nagato in Hiroshima Bay. His letter predicted an impending conflict between the United States and Great Britain. The admiral could see a slim chance of success in any conventional approach. This is because Japan could not prevail in a traditional battle against a country with such great industrial strength.

He devised his scheme, which he termed Operation Z or Operation Hawaii, out of sheer distress. Yamamoto remarked that entire Japan's forces would need to be unwaveringly committed to their mission, even if it meant giving their lives. If any of his fellow naval officers thought his idea was too hazardous, the admiral also addressed them. They must take into account the chance that the enemy will boldly strike their country, destroying their capital and other towns.

Yamamoto was confident that the deadly attack of Pearl Harbor would persuade America to cede Asia to Japan. It was a possibility when coupled with the urgent necessity to battle Hitler on the other side of the globe. Indeed, his fellow officers severely criticized his plan. According to Vice Admiral Chuichi Nagumo, Yamamoto's plan was ridiculous given the size of the American force, Oahu's location from the Japanese mainland, and the shallow waterways of Pearl Harbor.

On the other hand, some officers in the Imperial Japanese Navy believed Yamamoto's plan was absurd. It would astound the Americans—who in their right state of mind could ever conjure up such a plan? Its sole hope of success was there. They still anticipated losing a third of their task force's ships to defend against US bombers.

Isoroku Yamamoto then sent a more thorough proposition to the chief of staff of the Eleventh Air Fleet, Rear Admiral Takijiro Onishi, onboard the aircraft carrier Kaga, as a follow-up to his first ideas to the ministry. Yamamoto instructed Onishi to investigate if attacking the American base would be technically feasible. Onishi acquired as many details about Pearl Harbor as he could. Onishi consulted Commander Kosei Maeda, a specialist in aerial torpedo warfare. According to Maeda, a great fleet would find it incredibly challenging to go undetected from Japan to Hawaii.

On the other hand, Kaga's First Aerial Division staff officer, Minoru Genda, agreed that the plan was challenging but not unattainable. Rear Admiral Ryunosuke Kusaka, who was highly concerned about the area's air defenses, received the majority of Yamamoto's planning instructions. Kusaka was inspired by Yamamoto's reassurance that Pearl Harbor was his idea and that he needed Kusaka's help. Further, Genda stressed that the assault should be launched in the wee hours of the morning in complete secrecy, using an aircraft carrier force and various bombing techniques.

Pilots began severe training in Kagoshima City on Kyushu over the summer. Because of its location and infrastructure, it would simulate the same situations at Pearl Harbor, which is why Genda chose it. Each crew practiced flying over the 1,500-meter mountain behind Kagoshima before descending to 7.6 meters at the docks after avoiding buildings and smokestacks. Bombers fired torpedoes toward a breakwater some 270 meters away. Japanese armament engineers developed and tested modifications to enable successful low-water drops. By adding fins and release shackles to 356- and 406-mm naval rounds, Japanese weapons experts also created specialized armor-piercing bombs. These could get through the old warships' thinly armored decks.

Fun Fact:

Operation Z inception. When Japan won its first war with Russia, Isoroku Yamamoto was there. The 21-year-old ensign standing five feet three inches tall was onboard one of those torpedo boats charging the Russian navy in the Tsushima fogs. On May 27, 1905, Admiral Heihachiro Togo raised the Z flag atop his battleship, the Mikasa, just before confronting the Russian Baltic Fleet under Admiral Rozhestvensky. This inspired the Operation Z label, a symbol of a successful past.

Fun Fact:

Gendaism. Minoru Genda, 36, who was outstanding in the battles with China and the center of attention of Genda's Flying Circus, is as well-known as any movie star. He led a group of stunt pilots that did amazing aerial daredevilry. He was a significant figure in planning the attack on Pearl Harbor. Gendaism, the term for the naval use of aggressive airpower and an offensive stance emphasizing carriers, destroyers, and submarines, would become well-known in Japan.

Question:

1. Who planned the Pearl Harbor attack?

2. What did Admiral Chuichi Nagumo think of the Pearl Harbor attack plan?

3. What was the plan to attack Pearl Harbor called? Where was the name based from?

Answers:

1. Who planned the Pearl Harbor attack? **Admiral Isoroku**

2. What did Admiral Chuichi Nagumo think of the Pearl Harbor attack plan? **The plan was ridiculous.**

3. What was the plan to attack Pearl Harbor called? Where was the name based from? **Operation Z. It was based on the battle in Tsushima on May 27, 1905, when Admiral Heihachiro Togo raised the Z flag atop his battleship.**

THE PASSIVE AMERICAN DEFENSE

Coincidentally, Admiral James Otto Richardson memoed Chief of Naval Operations Harold Rainsford Stark in January 1941. The message concerned the fleet's defense and capacity to repel strikes the same month Yamamoto wrote his letter. Navy Secretary Frank Knox warned War Secretary Harold Stimson in a letter dated January 24 that a carrier assault of bombs or torpedoes would attack the fleet. Further, the attack could be made before the declaration of war without prior notice.

Two strategies were available to counter the attack—the first involved finding and eliminating the ship before unleashing jets. The second was to counter advancing bombers using fighters and anti-aircraft weapons. No long-range surveillance planes were available for the Navy component of the local defense forces that could be used to identify enemy carriers. When carriers were found, only Army bombers from the local air defense groups could attack them. For the reasons mentioned above, neither the quality nor the quantity of these Army bombers was sufficient.

Furthermore, the Army maintains 36 pursuit planes in the Hawaiian region that have all been deemed obsolete. Ideally, the district would have planes to guard against submarines, but none exist. General William L. Mitchell warned that airplanes would play a new role in future conflicts, particularly those with Japan, in attacking existing ships and installations in a 324-page document he wrote as early as 1924. Even though he raised the potential for an air attack on Pearl Harbor, his warnings went unheeded.

Although experiments had shown that shallow-water aircraft torpedo strikes were feasible, no one in control in Hawaii fully understood this. Moreover, American officials had been advised on the matter. Lord Louis Mountbatten, a British naval officer, traveled to Pearl Harbor in October 1941. He also informed Stark of the base's vulnerability to a bombing strike.

Decision-makers in Washington had access to information that was inconsistent, dispersed poorly, inconclusive, and lacked any supporting analysis. Nothing in it specifically suggested an attack on Pearl Harbor. The lack of knowledge about Imperial Navy capabilities contributed to the popular misconception that Pearl Harbor was not a likely target for a strike. All Pacific commanders, including the Navy and Army in Hawaii, received independent and unequivocal warnings late in November about an anticipated war with Japan in the near future. Also, it would be preferable for Japan to initiate hostilities first. Once more, it never raised the possibility of Pearl Harbor being the target.

Additionally, the Navy chose not to construct torpedo nets or barriers because they would interfere with routine operations. Moreover, they believed Pearl Harbor had built-in protections against torpedo attacks, such as the shallow water. The Army's preparedness status was also unclear due to General Walter Campbell Short's modification of local alert status designations without properly notifying Washington. The majority of the Army's mobile anti-aircraft weapons were guarded, and ammunition was kept locked up in armories. Guns were not scattered around Pearl Harbor out of respect for property owners and in accordance with Washington's warning not to alarm civil populations.

Fun Fact:

Three types of bombing. There were three methods of bombing—high-level horizontal, torpedo, and dive. As Minoru Genda intended to use fighters, as well as all three kinds of bombing, he requested every carrier in the Japanese navy to commit to Operation Z. The bombing should be carried out as an unexpected dawn attack. Japanese bombing capability was not yet advanced enough to launch attacks at night.

Fun Fact: .

Americans' perception of Japan. At this time, China was highly valued by the Americans. However, they had a low opinion of Japan, considering them racially inferior, slow-witted, illogical, unsophisticated, manic, obsessive, and mechanically incompetent. An essential contributing factor to the surprise at Pearl Harbor was the vast majority of Americans who could not fathom Japan assaulting the United States effectively.

Reflection Questions:

Admiral James Otto Richardson memoed Chief of Naval Operations Harold Rainsford Stark in January 1941. The message concerned the fleet's defense and capacity to repel strikes. Further, Navy Secretary Frank Knox warned War Secretary Harold Stimson in a letter dated January 24 that a carrier assault of bombs or torpedoes would attack the fleet. Further, the attack could be made before the declaration of war without prior notice. However, leaders ignored the warning resulting in unpreparedness in Pearl Harbor. **Leaders ignored the early reasonable warnings because of the perception that Pearl Harbor was not a likely target. Do you agree? Yes/No**

THE STRIKE

The damaged battleship at Pearl Harbor during the Japanese bombing.

Although it happened before Japan declared a formal declaration of war, Admiral Yamamoto did not intend this to happen. Initially, he stated that the strike should not start until 30 minutes after Japan had notified the US that peace talks had ended. Tokyo sent the 5000-word-two-block notice to the Japanese Embassy in Washington. The message's transcription took too long, preventing the Japanese embassy from delivering it on time. It was not disclosed until after the assault had started, which was more than an hour.

Under the direction of Commander Mitsuo Fuchida, the initial attack group of 183 aircraft was launched north of Oahu. Warships and naval ships were the first targets. Forty-nine Nakajima B5N Kate bombers with 800-kg armor-piercing explosives and 40 B5N bombers with Type 91 torpedoes were among the initial batch. Both were grouped into four divisions.

The US Army SCR-270 radio at Opana Point on the island's northern end picked up the first wave as it neared Oahu. Although this post had been in training for months, it needed to be in service. At the poorly staffed Intercept Center, Lieutenant Kermit A. Tyler, a freshly posted officer, assumed it was the anticipated entry of six B-17 bombers from California.

Several US warplanes were intercepted and destroyed as the initial wave of planes reached Oahu. At least one of them radioed a warning that was a little chaotic. The Japanese air assault started at 7:48 a.m., Hawaii Time (3:18 a.m. December 8, Japanese Standard Time). Other alerts from vessels off the harbor entrance were either still being assessed or awaiting approval.

In two waves, 353 Japanese aircraft arrived on Oahu. The first wave, headed by plodding, defenseless torpedo bombers, took advantage of the first shock to target the most significant battleships there. From the largest Hickam Field to Wheeler Field, the primary US Army Air Forces fighter facility, the dive bombers targeted US air units on Oahu. Approximately eight of the forty-nine 800-kg armor-piercing bombs dropped during the first wave of the attack struck their targeted battleships.

Lieutenant-Commander Shigekazu Shimazaki was in charge of the 171 airplanes that made up the second wave: 54 B5Ns, 81 D3As, and 36 A6Ms. A total of three groups of aircraft made up this wave and its objectives. One was ordered to assault Kāne'ohe, while the others were to the Pearl Harbor main. The targets included hangars, airplanes, carriers, cruisers, Ford Island, and Barbers Point. The different groups reached the attack point from multiple directions, almost all at the same time.

Only a few P-36 Hawks, P-40 Warhawks, and Scout Bomber Douglas (SBD) Dauntless dive bombers from the battleship Enterprise provided any aircraft combat. The defense was ill-prepared. Weapons were unattended, ammunition storage was closed, and airplanes were stationed wingtip to wingtip in the open to dissuade sabotage.

Despite being on low alert, a large number of American soldiers were able to respond efficiently during the attack. Although gravely injured, Ensign Joseph Taussig Jr. of Nevada Destroyer, who oversaw the ship's anti-aircraft guns, remained in his position. When the captain was absent from charge, Lt. Commander F. J. Thomas took over and moved the vessel until it grounded at 9:10 a.m. Captain Mervyn Bennion, in charge of West Virginia, led his men until he was killed by bomb shrapnel that struck Tennessee, anchored nearby. Only four soldiers, all ensigns, and none with more than a year's worth of sea service, were aboard one of the destroyers, Aylwin, as it set out.

Fun Fact:

Mock bombing. A squadron of aircraft flying in a V formation between the Army Air Corps base at Hickam and the navy's fortress of Pearl Harbor was spotted by Fred Kamaka, a 17-year-old student at Kamehameha High School. The Hawaiian locals thought the Japanese assault on Pearl Harbor was a mock bombing exercise. It was understandable as everyone had watched the army and navy perform interservice war simulations the week prior, which included a pretend attack on Honolulu Harbor.

Fun Fact:

No alarm on Kaneohe. It was a brand-new Naval Air Station in Kaneohe. The construction crew's steam siren on the contractor's clock inside the hut served as the station's improvised general alarm. It was Sunday during the Japanese attack; therefore, the shed was locked, and there was no steam for the whistle. There was no alarm at all.

True or False:

1. The attack happened before Japan formally declared war. Admiral Yamamoto intended for this to happen.

2. Japan attacked Pearl Harbor in three waves.

3. The Hawaiian locals thought the Japanese assault on Pearl Harbor was a mock bombing exercise.

4. Under the direction of Admiral Yamamoto, the initial attack group of 183 aircraft was launched north of Oahu.

5. The message's transcription took too long, but the Japanese embassy delivered it on time.

Answers:

1. The attack happened before Japan formally declared war. Admiral Yamamoto intended for this to happen. **False. Admiral Yamamoto did not intend for this to happen.**

2. Japan attacked Pearl Harbor in three waves. **False. Two waves.**

3. The Hawaiian locals thought the Japanese assault on Pearl Harbor was a mock bombing exercise. **True**

4. Under the direction of Admiral Yamamoto, the initial attack group of 183 aircraft was launched north of Oahu. **False. Commander Mitsuo Fuchida**

5. The message's transcription took too long, but the Japanese embassy delivered it on time. **False. The message was delivered more than an hour after the attack.**

LOSSES AND DAMAGE
TO AMERICANS

Burning and damaged ships at Pearl Harbor during the
Japanese assault.

The attack lasted for 90 agonizing minutes. Two thousand-eight sailors died, 710 were injured, 218 soldiers and airmen died, and 364 were hurt. 109 marines died, 69 were wounded, 68 civilians died, and 35 were hurt. In total, 2,403 Americans lost their lives, and 1,143 others were injured. Nearly half of the casualties among Americans were caused by the forward magazine blast of Arizona, which exploded after being struck by a modified 16-inch shell.

Technically, none of the Americans who died or were hurt in the attack were considered fighters because there were no active hostilities at the time. Junior enlisted soldiers made up the great majority of the US sailors lost at Pearl Harbor. All the Navy's officers resided in homes, while the junior personnel were on vessels.

Nine Honolulu Fire Department (HFD) firemen who attended Hickam Field during the attack in Honolulu were among the significant civilian victims. They became the first and only fire service members ever to have a foreign entity attack them while they were on American soil. They were firemen Harry Tuck Lee Pang, Captains Thomas Macy, and John Carreira, and six additional firemen injured by Japanese debris. They were awarded Purple Hearts, initially intended for military members injured during armed conflicts due to enemy activity.

Five battleships were among the 18 ships that came ashore or were sunk, damaged, and on fire amidships. The Destroyer

Nevada made an effort to leave the harbor despite being torpedo-damaged and on fire amidships. As she began to move, numerous Japanese bombers started to target her. It took further hits from 113-kg bombs, and other fires were set off. Apart from Nevada, Arizona, Oklahoma, West Virginia, California, Tennessee, Pennsylvania, and Maryland were among the battleships that were bombed.

Despite focusing on battleships, the largest ships on the scene, the Japanese did not disregard other targets. The cruisers, a type of warship, were among the targets. The cruisers Helena, Raleigh, and Honolulu, were torpedoed. The destroyers were also not missed by the Japanese. A destroyer is a quick, agile, and long-lasting warship designed to accompany larger ships in a squadron, convoy, or battle group and protect them against solid short-range assaults. The destroyers Cassin, Helm, Downes, and Shaw were hit by bombs or caught fire.

There were 402 American planes in Hawaii- 155 of them were on the ground while 188 of them were wrecked, and 159 were disfigured. During the raid, eight Army Air Forces fighters were able to take off. However, nearly none were genuinely prepared to depart to protect the base. Nine civilian planes were also flying near Pearl Harbor, and three were taken down.

Japanese Casualties

The operation resulted in the deaths of 55 Japanese flyers and nine submariners and the capture of one, Kazuo Sakamaki. Three hundred fifty of Japan's 414 available aircraft participated in the strike, which destroyed 29 aircraft. During the initial wave, three pilots, one dive bomber, and five torpedo bombers perished. Six planes and fourteen dive bombers were lost in the second wave. Additional 74 planes were damaged by ground-based anti-aircraft fire.

Fun Fact:

Hospitals were spared. The Japanese pilots will always be honored for not bombing the hospital. An enormous red cross on the roof served as a blatant marker for the structure. If they had, there would have been a horrible massacre. Several rescuers and injured people had gathered inside and around it.

Fun Fact: .

Ration of milk. Everyone in the Schofield Barracks for the Army was pleased to get their half-pint of milk every Sunday. The soldiers were more focused on obtaining and retaining their milk ration than they were on hearing the approaching explosions. It just proves that the strike was unexpected.

Encircle the Correct Word

1. The attack lasted for **60/90** agonizing minutes.

2. **Junior enlisted soldiers**/**Navy officers** made up the great majority of the US sailors lost at Pearl Harbor.

3. **Five/Nine** Honolulu Fire Department (HFD) firemen who attended Hickam Field were among the significant civilian victims.

4. Everyone in the Schofield Barracks for the Army was pleased to get their half-pint of **milk/beer** every Sunday.

Answers:

1. The attack lasted for **90** agonizing minutes.

2. **Junior enlisted soldiers** made up the great majority of the US sailors lost at Pearl Harbor.

3. **Nine** Honolulu Fire Department (HFD) firemen who attended Hickam Field were among the significant civilian victims.

4. Everyone in the Schofield Barracks for the Army was pleased to get their half-pint of **milk** every Sunday.

RECOVERY OF PEARL HARBOR AND DECLARATION OF WARS

Pearl Harbor during the surprise strike by the Japanese in December 1941.

On December 8, 1941, a Joint Session of Congress heard President Roosevelt's Day of Infamy address. He urged a formal declaration of war against the Empire of Japan- the day after the Pearl Harbor attack. Shortly on that same day, Congress declared war on Germany and Italy. Germany and Italy proclaimed war on the United States on December 11, even if it was unnecessary, as per the Tripartite Pact.

Japan struck the Philippines a few hours later, on December

8 in the Philippines, due to the time difference. The United Kingdom was already in conflict with Germany since September 1939 and Italy since June 1940. British Prime Minister Winston Churchill had pledged to wage war shortly after the Japanese attacked the United States. The Japanese were already assaulting Malaya, Singapore, and Hong Kong. Consequently, the UK proclaimed war on Japan nine hours ahead of the United States.

Prince of Wales and Repulse battleships were lost off the coast of Malaya just three days following the Pearl Harbor attack. Churchill said he had never experienced a more direct jolt during the war. He claimed that Japan was in charge of this large body of water and that everyone else was helpless and exposed.

Residents and citizens of Japan in America also suffered the consequences of the assault on Pearl Harbor. They were transferred to detention facilities for Japanese Americans. Further, several Japanese-American officials were apprehended and transported to high-security camps within hours of the attack. Under the War Measures Act, the

Government of Canada permitted the forcible expulsion of all Canadians of Japanese heritage from British Columbia and the prohibition of their return. Hundreds of thousands of Japanese immigrants were sent to camps or forced to work on farms.

In Pearl Harbor, Captain Homer N. Wallin was assigned to oversee a thorough recovery operation following an extensive search for survivors. Divers from the Navy, the Pearl Harbor Naval Shipyard, and private contractors started working on the vessels that could be returned to service in the area of Pearl Harbor. Five battleships and two cruisers were repaired or refloated in six months to be transported to Pearl Harbor and mainland facilities for in-depth restoration.

Weapons and gear were removed from damaged ships that couldn't be repaired and used on other boats. Vigorous recovery activities persisted for a total of 20,000 person-hours below waters over the course of another year. Battleship Arizona became a memorial site. Utah, the target vessel, was too severely damaged to be salvaged and is still at sea. The American aircraft carriers, to the country's benefit, remained unharmed.

Pearl Harbor immediately after the Japanese attack, taken by a Naval photographer.

The Japanese attack successfully achieved its goal but was ultimately completely unnecessary. Unknown to Yamamoto, who originally planned the attack, the US Navy had already resolved to forgo marching across the Pacific for the Philippines in reaction to a war's breakout as early as 1935. The Japanese disregarded Pearl Harbor's navy maintenance facilities, oil tank farms, submarine base, and former headquarters building. They believed they could quickly secure a victory. Repair and fuel storage facilities continued to exist, allowing Pearl Harbor to continue providing logistical support for US Navy operations.

Pearl Harbor was widely referenced in American propaganda throughout the period. Propaganda is the intentional distribution of carefully selected facts, opinions, or rumors, usually intending to uphold a nation's self-interest.

Fun Fact:

Japanese-American camps. Driven by the paranoia of another surprise attack, the Japanese-Americans were sent to relocation camps in California, Arizona, Wyoming, Idaho, Utah, Texas, Colorado, and Arkansas. They were kept in improvised camps surrounded by barbed wire and watchtowers in the desert or the highlands. The children in one of the camps began each day by reciting the flag's Pledge of Allegiance. A flag of the United States could be seen in the center of the camp.

Fun Fact:

Japanese-American camps. Driven by the paranoia of another surprise attack, the Japanese-Americans were sent to relocation camps in California, Arizona, Wyoming, Idaho, Utah, Texas, Colorado, and Arkansas. They were kept in improvised camps surrounded by barbed wire and watchtowers in the desert or the highlands. The children in one of the camps began each day by reciting the flag's Pledge of Allegiance. A flag of the United States could be seen in the center of the camp.

Match the Year/Date with the Events

Events	Date/Year
Japan struck the Philippines,	April 18, 1943
Germany, and Italy proclaimed war on the United States	December 8, 1941
President Roosevelt's Day of Infamy address	December 8
Assassination of Admiral Yamamoto	December 11

Answers:

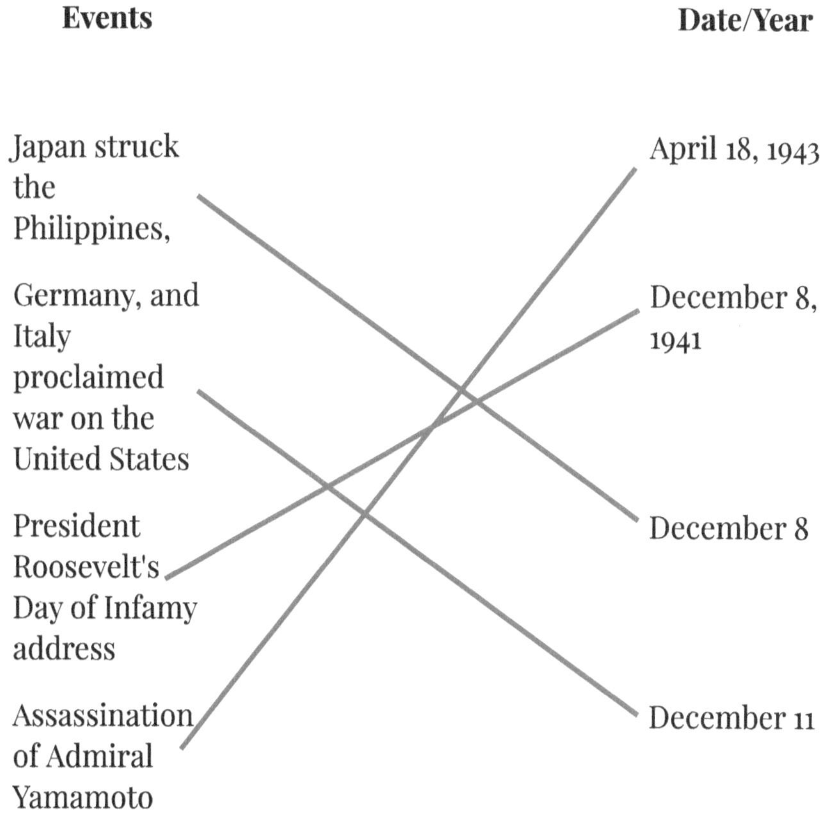

Pearl Harbor

CONCLUSION

"We won a great tactical victory at Pearl Harbor and thereby lost the war."

– Admiral Chuichi Hara

Wars can grow and shatter empires, bring an end to nations, and create new ones. They may also take countless lives, demolish cultures and peoples, and destroy entire civilizations. War, however, can also inspire scientific advancement, win the freedom of captives, and reveal the patriotism, conviction, and bravery that can exist in regular people.

Humanity appears to be at its most vicious, deadly, and aggressively worst during the war. However, Stanford scholar Ian Morris says warfare has also contributed to world peace and progress. Japanese pilots omitting the hospitals as bomb targets already says much about these soldiers. Despite the horrible number of deaths, the sense of humanity was never lost.

The emotions evoked by war range from awe to terror. One cannot help but empathize with the Japanese knowing the inequality they experienced. Simultaneously, the massacre they committed while expanding territories was unforgivable. Even with powerful countries like America, colonizing other countries might elicit resentment. However, colonization positively impacts technology, education, and medical science.

Further, America underestimating Japan's capability to attack Pearl Harbor was a compelling point. The arrogance of the American leaders at that time led to numerous fatalities in Pearl Harbor. Had they heeded the warnings, the attack would not have been a surprise. Several lives were lost in Pearl Harbor due to unpreparedness. A few of the personnel were even asleep during the attack.

While there are many heroes in the Pearl Harbor story, some of the most important ones went unnoticed until this point. After the fires at Pearl Harbor were put out, war workers began saving alongside military troops. Five thousand separate dives, totaling twenty thousand hours undersea, were needed for the recovery work. Even though these men could not revive the deceased, they miraculously repaired everything with speed and intensity.

BIBLIOGRAPHY

- Pearl Harbor on December 7, 1941, when Japan launched a devastating surprise offensive on the US Pacific Fleet. During the assault, two bombs and six torpedoes sank West Virginia.

  "Pearl Harbor" by The U.S. Army is licensed under CC BY 2.0. To view a copy of this license, visit https://creativecommons.org/licenses/by/2.0/?ref=openverse.

- Pearl Harbor immediately after the Japanese attack, taken by a Naval photographer.

  "Public Domain: WWII: Pearl Harbor Attack (NARA)" by pingnews.com is marked with Public Domain Mark 1.0. To view the terms, visit https://creativecommons.org/publicdomain/mark/1.0//?ref=openverse.

- Pearl Harbor during the surprise strike by the Japanese in December 1941.

  "Public Domain: WWII: Pearl Harbor Attack (NARA)" by pingnews.com is marked with Public Domain Mark 1.0. To view the terms, visit https://creativecommons.org/publicdomain/mark/1.0/?ref=openverse.

- Burning and damaged ships at Pearl Harbor during the Japanese assault.

  "Pearl Harbor, 7 December 1941" by Archives Branch, USMC History Division is licensed under CC BY 2.0. To view a copy of this license, visit https://creativecommons.org/licenses/by/2.0/?ref=openverse.

- The damaged battleship at Pearl Harbor during the Japanese bombing.

  "Public Domain: Pearl Harbor Damage (NARA)" by pingnews.com is marked with Public Domain Mark 1.0. To view the terms, visit https://creativecommons.org/publicdomain/mark/1.0/?ref=openverse.

- Pearl Harbor, the location of the Japanese air raid that brought America into World War II, may be seen on the bottom left side of the photo. The harbor continues to be a base for the US navy.

  "Pearl Harbor, Hawaii" by NASA Goddard Photo and Video is licensed under CC BY 2.0. To view a copy of this license, visit https://creativecommons.org/licenses/by/2.0/?ref=openverse.

- General Douglas MacArthur, President Franklin D. Roosevelt, and Admiral Chester W. Nimitz, in Pearl Harbor 1944.

  "Roosevelt - MacArthur - Nimitz in Pearl Harbor - Hawaii - 1944" by Marion Doss is licensed under CC BY-SA 2.0. To view a copy of this license, visit https://creativecommons.org/licenses/by-sa/2.0/?ref=openverse.

About Us

At our core, we believe that history is more than just a subject to be learned. It's an experience to be had.

Our mission is to educate and inspire the next generation by providing them with a window into the fascinating and often surprising world of the past. We want to help young people make sense of the complexities of history and understand the lessons it has to offer.

By creating unforgettable encounters with relics of the past, we hope to ignite a lifelong passion for learning and discovery.

Thank you,